Origins

Dragon Hunter

Claire Llewellyn
Character illustrations by Jonatronix

Contents

OXFORD
UNIVERSITY PRESS

Dragon stories

About 100 years ago, people began to hear stories about real-life dragons. The dragons lived on an island called *Komodo*.

An **explorer** in New York heard about the dragons. He wanted to go to Komodo. He wanted to find out if the stories were true. His name was *W Douglas Burden*.

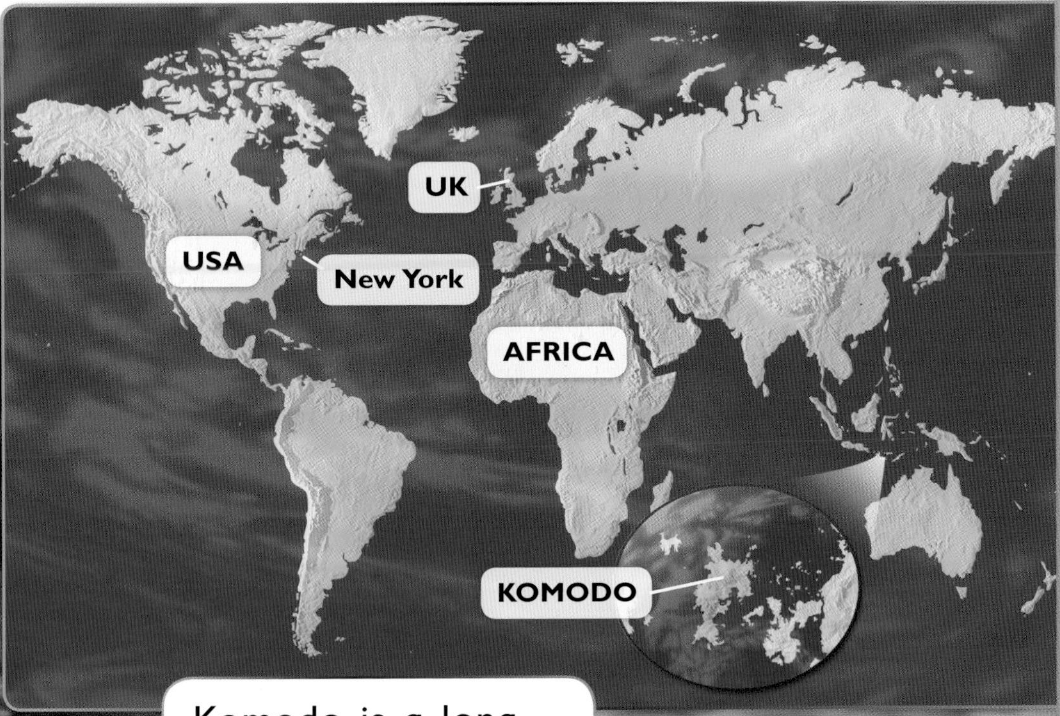

Komodo is a long way from New York.

The island of Komodo

Burden sailed to Komodo. He took a team of people with him. He wanted to catch a dragon and take it back to New York.

Burden had to share his shelter with spiders and snakes!

When Burden and his team got to the island they made a shelter. Then they went to look for the dragons.

Discovering the dragon

Burden explored the island. He saw a huge footprint in the mud. Then he heard a noise … He looked up and saw a giant beast.

Its head moved from side to side. It had sharp teeth and claws. It had a long forked tongue. Burden had **discovered** a dragon!

A dragon trap

Burden called the beast a *Komodo dragon*. He wanted to catch one to take back to New York. So he and his team made a trap. They put a dead goat inside.

Do you think it's right to trap a wild animal?

A huge Komodo dragon came to eat the goat. The dragon got stuck in the trap. Burden locked it in a cage but the dragon was very strong. The next day, it had gone.

Dragons in New York

In the end, Burden trapped two smaller dragons. He took them back to New York and gave them to a zoo. He gave some dead dragons to a **museum**. The museum put the dragons on show.

You can still see Burden's dragons today. They are on show in the *Museum of Natural History*, New York.

Burden told lots of people about his adventure. One of those people made a film. It was about an explorer who took a giant beast to New York. The film was called *King Kong*.

Have you seen any films about monsters?

A scene from the film *King Kong*, 1933.

Komodo dragons

Komodo dragons are giant **lizards**. They use their tongues to taste the air. This helps them to find food.

Komodo dragons are dangerous. Their mouths are full of deadly **germs**. If they bite an animal, the germs will kill it. The dragons sometimes bite and kill people too.

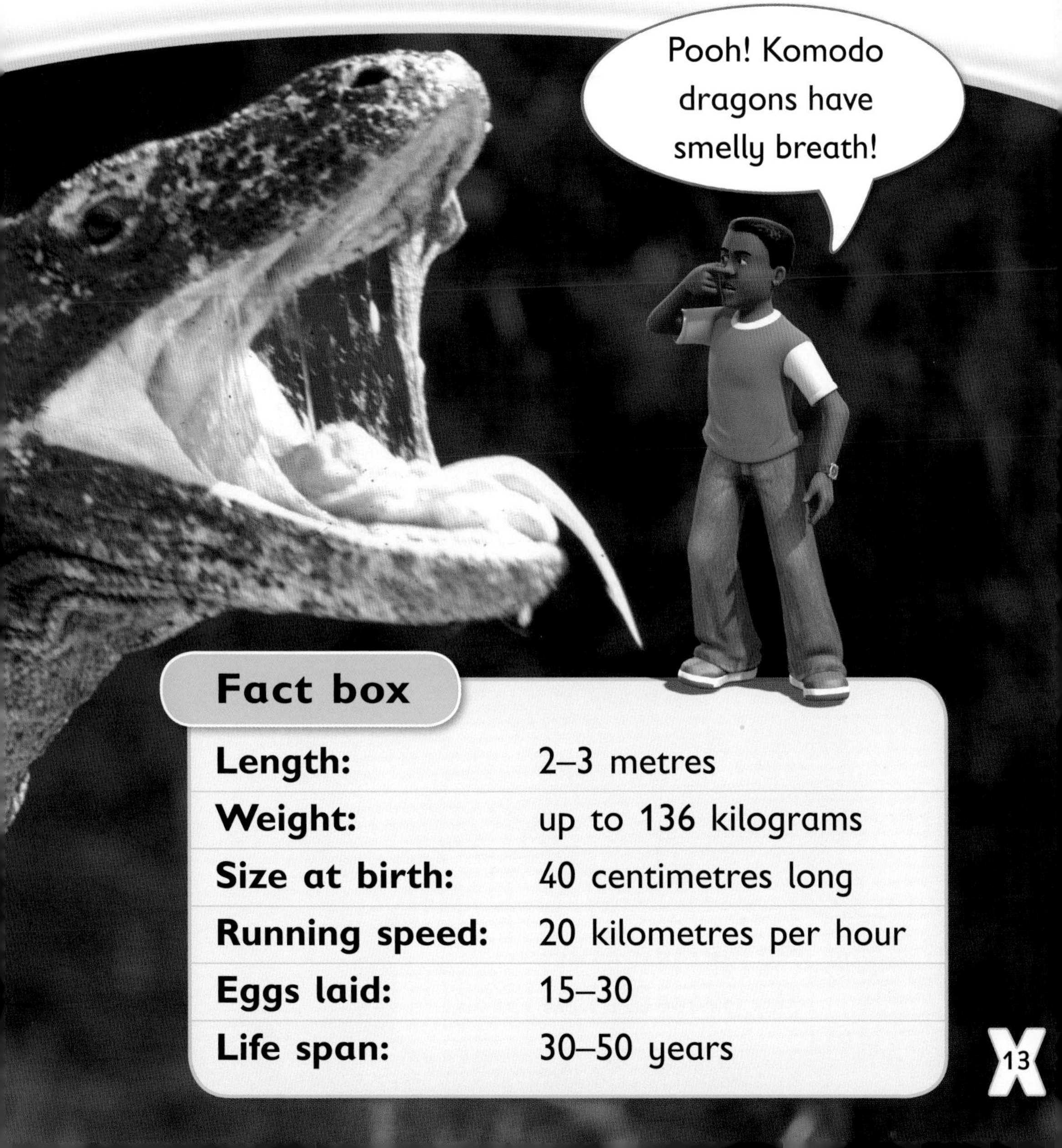
Pooh! Komodo dragons have smelly breath!

Fact box

Length:	2–3 metres
Weight:	up to 136 kilograms
Size at birth:	40 centimetres long
Running speed:	20 kilometres per hour
Eggs laid:	15–30
Life span:	30–50 years

New discoveries

Komodo dragons still live on Komodo. There are about 5000 dragons alive today. Are there any other animals still to be discovered? Yes! All these animals have been discovered in the last few years.

Purple sea star – discovered in America.

Discovered

Yariguies brush-finch – discovered in South America.

Discovered

Highland mangabey – discovered in Africa.

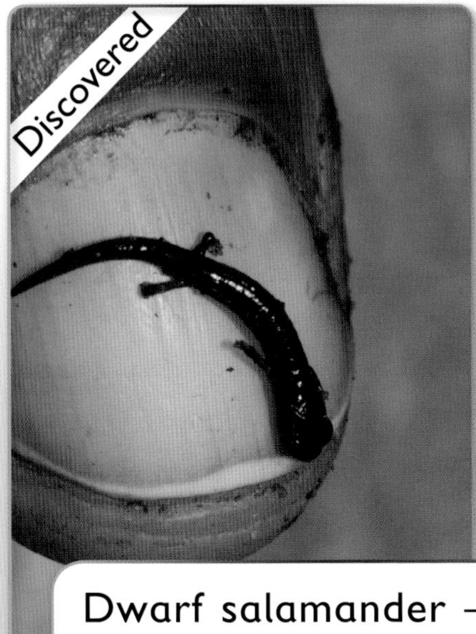
Discovered

If you were an explorer, what kind of animal would you like to find?

Dwarf salamander – discovered in South America.

Glossary

discover to find out about something

explorer a person who travels to places that we know little about

germ a tiny living thing, too small to see. Some germs can make you sick

lizard an animal with scaly skin

museum a place where interesting things are kept for people to go and see

Index